D. M.'

Flight and Smoke

Other titles by D. M. Thomas

Novels
The Flute-Player
Birthstone
The White Hotel
Russian Nights Quintet:
Ararat
Swallow
Sphinx
Summit
Lying Together
Flying in to Love
Pictures at an Exhibition
Eating Pavlova
Lady with a Laptop
Charlotte

Poetry
Penguin Modern Poets 11
Two Voices
Logan Stone
Love and Other Deaths
The Honeymoon Voyage
Dreaming on Bronze
The Puberty Tree: Selected Poems
Dear Shadows
Not Saying Anything
Unknown Shores: Collected SF Poems

Translations
Akhmatova: Selected Poems
Pushkin: Selected Poems

Memoirs
Memories and Hallucinations
Bleak Hotel

Biography
Alexander Solzhenitsyn: A Century in his Life

Play
Hell Fire Corner

Children's Fiction
The Devil and the Floral Dance

D. M. Thomas

Flight and Smoke

Poems

First published by Francis Boutle Publishers
272 Alexandra Park Road
London N22 7BG
Tel/Fax: 020 8889 7744
Email: info@francisboutle.co.uk
www.francisboutle.co.uk

Flight and Smoke © D. M. Thomas 2010

All rights reserved.
No part of this book may be reproduced, stored
in a retrieval system, or transmitted, in any form
or by any means, electronic, mechanical photocopying
or otherwise without the prior permission of the publishers.

ISBN 978 1 903427 52 1

Printed in Malta at Melita Press

Contents

Travelling with a Photographer

    6 Bright Star
    7 John Moyle
    9 An Alpine Night
  11 Hence Those Tears
  12 Bolsheviks
  13 The Contract
  15 The Half-Rhyme
  16 Anna Freud in the Blitz
  18 A Jewish Triptych
        Three Sisters
        Poland 1941
        In Theresienstadt
  21 Twelve Men's Moor
  22 Dover beach is located in europe
  24 Moth
  25 Shall I Compare You
  26 Learning to Translate
  28 Oxford Sabbatical
  29 Cricket Lover
  30 My Mistress' Eyes
  31 Floods
  32 Sweet Love, Renew thy Force
  33 In Cimino's *The Deer Hunter*
  34 Travelling with a Photographer

The Barbecue

  38 Suspender Belts

39 When Most I Wink
40 Flight and Smoke
42 Through the Fens
43 Check-in, Milan Airport
44 An English Wedding in Provence
47 Dachas
49 Images
50 The Barbecue
51 Since You Came
52 Cloudburst
53 'I never died, said he...'
55 After Christopher Smart
56 Sunday Morning on Madeira
57 Air Excess
59 Three Triolets:
    Obby Oss
    Latin Class
    Vermeer's Milkmaid
60 Centenary Thanksgiving for Thomas Merritt
62 Easter Reading
63 Changing the Flowers
65 A Kind of Relative
66 Mad Fathers
67 Schrödinger's Cat
69 Plain Song

Acknowledgements

After Christopher Smart first appeared in my memoir *Bleak Hotel* (Quartet books, 2008). A Jewish Triptych and Hinc Illae Lachrymae first appeared in the magazine *HQ*. An earlier version of Centenery Service for Thomas Merritt appeared in *Poetry Cornwall*. Three poems, previously uncollected, first appeared in anthologies: Moth and In Cimino's *The Deer Hunter* in *Over the Bridge*, edited by John Loveday (Kestrel Books, 1981); and Twelve Men's Moor in *The Puffin Book of Magic Verse*, edited by Charles Causley (Penguin, 1974). A slightly longer version of Travelling with a Photographer first appeared as an introductory poem to a book of photographs, *The Red River*, by Jem Southam (Copperhouse Publications, 1989).

DMT
Truro, Cornwall, 2010

www.dmthomasonline.net

Travelling with a Photographer

Bright Star

I'm afraid I read trashy, trumpety novels; art
Does not obsess me or Mr Lindon either.
Does hair turn grey when it's somewhere else, apart?
I've read his letters when I've lain sleepless.
They're very moving; he loved me so much,
Though quite violently. Thank God I stayed pure
For Mr Lindon. His friend showed me his death-mask:
Weird – his face, yet it bore no resemblance
To the young poet I allowed to stroke my breast
Once; and felt him swell… well, you know – men.
Hearing him cough next door, I couldn't rest…
'Tender is the night'… That's in an Ode;
I remember that. I'd be Mrs Keats if he'd lived.

Fanny Brawne (1800–1865), Keats's fiancée, married a sales agent, Louis Lindon, and bore him three children. Keats had a lock of her hair buried with him in Rome.

John Moyle

Soon after Sabbath midnight, he would rise
From a short rest, and leave his sleeping farm
And family, Alpine to Salt Lake,
Twenty two miles as the crow flies,
But John Moyle walked it in the holy night,
Praising God's purifying cold, the inward light.

And praised Him too for bringing him so far;
This walk mere child's play after the handcart
He'd pulled from Iowa to Utah earlier,
The weight of that had dragged back on his heart
Much like the drag back to the home he'd left,
Cornwall; a mother smiling, waving, and bereft.

Night, crumbling like sandstone, lifting like
A bridal dress, till he glimpsed the Lord's resplendent
New temple in the desert. Was never late
Arriving, the whistle summoning all at eight;
Emptied his bag of hammer, pasty, chisel, spike,
Becoming John Moyle, stonemason, superintendent.

Scorched like the lizards, he laid stone on stone;
Carved moons in phases, showing how we thrive
From birth to resurrection; shaped a One
All-seeing Eye. Fridays, packed up at five
And set off home, arriving by midnight,
His wife to greet him with the lantern's light.

All the next day he'd labour on his farm
Beneath a mountain, helped animals to birth,
And did his best, at night, for human love
To bring another soul to this good earth.
Sundays he sang hymns, led impromptu prayers.
Then out to blizzards or skies dense with stars.

Until one Saturday a bolting cow
At milking kicked him, shattering the leg-bone.

No help around; the farm marooned by snow;
A son unhinged a door and strapped him down,
Then with a bucksaw that had lopped a tree
Sawed off his shattered leg below the knee.

The doctor came at last, and shook his head.
Brethren rode out from Salt Lake, prayed, and sighed.
There was an hour his family thought he'd died;
But he was Jacob wrestling, his eyes closed;
Sat up one day, ate broth, and asked for wood
And tools; shaped himself a leg; shakily rose.

Each step a scream, he faltered round the house;
Later, rejoicing in a fierce wind, the yard;
And finally, with a pasty for his croust,
Limped all the way from Alpine to Salt Lake,
Where he climbed scaffolding, and with his spike
Carved in the red stone 'Holiness to the Lord'.

My son, alone with his laptop by a Thai pool,
Writing, with that ancestral joy in toil,
Though with Thai curries, chanced upon this Moyle
And was so moved by him he chose to end
An email with 'God bless our mighty forefathers'
Instead of his more usual ending, 'Cool'.

An Alpine Night

He signed the register, '*Dr Sigm Freud*
u frau.' In fading light the concierge saw
a mature couple, bourgeois Viennese,
flushed from the Alpine walking they'd enjoyed;
the wife, no beauty... He searched the row of keys,
then led Freud and, in fact, his sister-in-law,

Minna, upstairs and through a corridor.
He *lederhosen*ed, she in a stout skirt,
stepped carefully, rough paths still haunting them;
the Swiss put in his key, opened the door,
and ushered them into a murky room;
Freud answered his 'goodnight', and the door shut.

What happened after that, we've no idea.
Perhaps they lay apart, like sister with brother;
perhaps it was all one to him, Rachel or Leah,
bonded too close for sex to feel like sin,
or joy, or make either sister jealous when
he entered, from custom or courtesy, the other.

She told Jung, late in life, he'd been in love
with her, and it was troubling – so Jung said.
In which case he embraced her instantly,
then they laughed joyously, for one night free;
tore off each other's clothes, fell on the bed,
and were one tingling hand, one silken glove.

But I can see them, too, agreeing this
was sensible, saving expense. He stroked
the Roman god he'd bought, a real find;
to his companion, half-undressing, blind;
pecked on her almost-sleeping face a kiss,
then wrote a card to Martha while he smoked.

Whatever happened, or his wife supposed,
the sweet, majestic night had just begun;

no sooner had his eyes on blackness closed,
a woman coiled with him; he lay beneath;
his gaze entranced by her: Jocasta, death,
and his young Jewish mother, all in one.

Minna Bernays, a spinster, lived with the Freuds and their six children. The hotel entry for a night in August 1898 was found in 2006.

Hence Those Tears

Girls were like ghosts, till, after that last speech day,
He might admire a sister of a friend
And write to her, their friendship growing each day
Sweet summer glided towards a brutal end.

Then the boys wrote of England, School and Beauty –
Loyalties all Greek to us today;
Girls dreaded telegrams, but knew that Duty
Meant death would often be the manlier way.

For him, a blur – house-prizes, easy wickets,
Planning to meet in Cambridge after the vac,
Yelling at Northern lads, stunted from rickets,
To close ranks and press on with the attack.

Perhaps one home leave: meeting at St Pancras
First-class ladies' waiting-room, then stiff
Betrothal days; boys who'd been wankers
In their dorms, raised on reticence and *If*,

And their prim girls – some of whom exploded,
Within, from one late kiss, clumsy and shy –
Went back relieved to tender letters, coded
To warn of battle – *'hinc illae lachrymae'*:

'Hence those tears.' Many became like brothers,
Servants would write, and loved by all the men:
Sending a bloodstained tunic to a mother;
And to a girl her gifts – Shelley, a fountain pen:

And often verse, whose simple lines reveal
Their love of gentle English sights and scents,
An England never real, nor quite unreal,
And, dying too, that touching innocence.

Bolsheviks

Bolsheviks move around, like the medieval papacy,
from country to country.
'The eternal lightning of Lenin's bones'
can be generated by wind-farms and solar panels,
the cruelty of 'man is a wolf to man'
can turn into vegetarianism.

They may even take on the name
of a previous enemy, like
the various kinds of Democrats
before the October Revolution.

But they are always with us,
like the poor:
the Commissars and the technocrats
who decide what is good for the masses
and who deserve their privileges,
their special stores, schools, hospitals,
their fine apartments and *dachas*,
because they are serving the people.

They are always with us,
the *intelligentsia*
deciding our belief system
we can dissent from only in whispers;
always the Stalin awards for conformity.

There is always, unfortunately,
the idiot peasantry,
the stupid old *babushka*,
who continues to light candles
in empty village churches
and mumble her prayers at night
before she talks to her dead husband.

The Contract

(Vienna, 1930s)

You see the woman in the white silk suit
and boa – in that highly solemn four?
She makes a handsome living out of bridge.
A real pro... *Let's see, I'll bid one heart...*
Jewish, of course. Has an intriguing past;
she's Ida Bauer, 'Dora' in Freud's famous case.

I treated Bauer, her rich father, for a case
of – well, if I said, he'd slap a legal suit
on me. His wife turned cold, since he had passed
the virus on; so Bauer went hunting for
fresh meat. And found it in a Frau Stein's starved heart.
The couples had met on holiday – thanks to bridge.

The new lovers acted as if this *were* bridge.
They needed Herr Stein distracted, off the case.
Well, here was Ida, fifteen, stirred his heart;
grabbed by him, she felt – something – through his suit...
scared her. Freud thought she still craved it, four
years later, causing breathlessness... *I pass...*

Frau Stein wooed her too; I think it went past
sex-talk in bed and teaching the girl bridge;
there are more ways than one of making up a four
with a young girl. Herr Stein gave her a jewel-case
by a lake, then indecently pressed home his suit,
saying he'd divorce his wife... *Three hearts.*

What Ida longed for was her father's heart.
He trumped her, he finessed her... *You've passed,
and yet you must have honours in that suit...*
She dreamt, for Freud, a fire in which she bridged
father and seducer through a scorched jewel-case
that only papa could rescue... *I'll go four*

spades... Now, at long last, she exposed Stein for
an abuser; and he, hand on heart,
said it was Ida's fantasy, a sad case
of sex-mania; and Bauer believed him... *Pass*...
So can you see why she was drawn to bridge,
and why there's ice now under her nice suit?

And Freud? He said her marrying Stein would suit
everyone. She told him to jump off the Rudolf Bridge
and stormed out. Jews, eh? They're all heart!

The speaker's knowledge is not entirely accurate; the Steins (called by Freud the 'K's') were really called Zellenka.

The Half-Rhyme

The first word of my father's I remember
Came on a starlit night, outside our house,
When I was four – sometime before September
Of '39. The talk had been so serious
No one had seen me leave my pouff
To stamp on a spider crossing our lounge floor.
My hand gripped, as we watched his pal drive off,
I asked him, 'Daddy, is it peace or war?'
His strong voice calmed me: 'Peace'.

                              When he was dying,
My hand-clasp seemed too small a thing to give;
I said, choked up, 'Maureen is pregnant', lying,
But desperate to make him want to live.
Struggling against his stroke, he managed, 'Nice'.
And so we comforted each other, twice.

Anna Freud in the Blitz

Those young Luftwaffe men up there – I still
can't bring myself to hate them, even though
they try to kill us. My dear, I pity them;
they're frightened too. Some on this raid tonight
may long to see the Ringstrasse again
as I do; yearn to be back home, as I do.
Except Vienna would not be my home
without you. Home is the mountain where you stood
last night, calling for me.

                       I never told you this:
I think I may have talked to the young Hitler.
When I was still a schoolgirl, walking home,
passing the Jewish pedlars from the East,
I stopped before one of them, who sold postcards
with his own sketches of the city on them.
I stopped because his eyes attracted me,
intense, light-blue. Only your eyes, papa,
were more intense. I thought him Jewish too,
same long and ragged coat, long sallow face,
and big feet made for desert walking; but
he spoke in rustic German, not in Yiddish.
He looked so desperate and starved, I bought
one of his cards, showing the Opera;
not bad, not good. He told me he loved music.
I've read he looked quite Jewish in Vienna.
...That bomb fell close, it shook the Gradiva
askew, I'll go and straighten it... and have a pee...

                    Then I saw him again,
bumped into him after the Karl May lecture,
his eyes aglow from all that idealism –
pacifism and a nobler world. I felt it too;
we neither of us wanted to go home:
he to his workers' hostel, I to all our
comfort and culture. So we had coffee.
I never told you or mama. I should be punished.

He told me how his father, coming home drunk,
would thrash him. '*Beat, beat, beat*', that's how he put it,
and calling out each blow: '*nine, ten, eleven…*'
Papa, I got excited, I felt a warmth
around my lap, as though I'd spilt my coffee.
It won't surprise you; you know me so well.
How terribly ironic, I thought: he loathed
his almost nightly thrashing, whereas I –
I fantasised about being thrashed by you,
who were the gentlest father in the world!

He wanted to be an architect, to create
wonderful cities for the workers, with
lots of green space… That bomb was further off;
now he's creating spaces, here in London!…
I felt ashamed, hearing his fine ideas
while I was warm and weak from that all-flooding
sensation. I paid for our coffees, also
a *torte* for him, and had to ask mama
for extra pocket money that week, saying
I'd bought a birthday gift for a schoolfriend.

I feel sure there was good in him, just as
there's evil, all too much of it, in me.
If I had had his background, and he mine…
Don't you think there's so much chance involved,
as to which side of the river, so to speak,
we're cast ashore on?

                     – That's the all-clear,
thank God. I hope the children are all safe.
I'll make a warm drink, and then try to sleep.
Goodnight, my dear one.

After Freud's death in London in 1939, his daughter Anna treated children who had suffered in the Blitz. Karl May: a German pacifist romance-writer.

A Jewish Tryptich

Three Sisters

He aligned the heads carefully,
like the true artist he was,
one behind the other; gently tilted
a chin, a cheek, with his gloved finger,
as a hairdresser might.
Everything had to be perfect
for this still life on a cold
but invigorating day.
He would remember this forever…
Three sisters… That fucking Jewish
teacher he'd had for a time –
hadn't he taught some stupid play
by that name? Well, let's say this
was his German epilogue
to it. The heads remained still,
as he lit a cigarette between cupped hands
and took a deep draw. Then he shot them all
with the one shot. 'Please, we're sisters,'
they had begged; 'let us die together.'
He had nodded, happy to blend
kindness with expertise.
One sister screamed when she
was thrown into the fire,
but you can't expect perfection.

(An incident at Auschwitz)

Poland 1941

On a warm evening, after a forest clearance,
Stress ebbed away. The girl who cleaned for him
Brought him his schnapps outside – also somehow
A purity that touched him, and he said,

'You're very nice. I'll never kill you with
The others.' Showed her then a flowering tree
Of a rare beauty. 'I'll kill you separately
And put you under it.' As she withdrew,

He thought: 'I haven't lost my decent heart.'
By chance she lived; an artist now in London.
The catalogues say 'born in Poland', and
When browsers gaze at a rich flowering tree

In her 'Self Portrait, Childhood Memories',
They sense romantic Chopin in her art,
And try to guess the tender memory.

Alicia Adams, sole survivor of 30,000 in her town. 'Forest clearance' – a mass killing.

In Theresienstadt

One had to find some joy
even in such a hell.
One way was Verdi's Requiem;
and the Nazis who clapped
never imagined the *Dies Irae*
could apply to *them*!
But the most joyous memory
– remember, we were well-brought-up
Jewish girls, separated from
Our husbands! – was in our room.
Twelve of us slept there, but often
there were twelve men too!
Sex aching all through.

We never looked aside or even
listened; and yet

so powerful an experience
is impossible to forget,
and with my second husband
when I felt the tides of desire
recede in me,
I'd set myself on fire
by imagining those twelve men
were sowing their seed in me.

It was the only way to be fulfilled:
Through that dark fantasy.
Only this time, unlike then,
one's baby would not be killed
or at least left to die
as happened to me.

It can still happen, if I'm honest;
though I'm old and by myself,
I can bring the dead to life,
A baby, and those twelve men
soon for the transport
out of that haven, Theresienstadt.

Twelve Men's Moor

(North Cornwall)

Who shaped me like a cromlech?
Who holed me like a crickstone?
Who rocked me like a logan?
Who enchanted me like ninemaidens?
Who blessed me like a holywell?
Who bloodied me like a tinstream?
Who lit me like a wrecker's lantern?
Who blinded me like an engine-house?
Who corroded me like an arsenic-flue?
Who deepened me like a shaft?
Who emptied me like a chapel?
Who built me and left me like scaffolding?

Dover beach is located in europe

(based on a student's critique of 'Dover Beach' on a website, 'uniqueskills.com')

Dover beach is located in europe,
this is not some honeymoon vacation in florida,
Arnolds is writin bout the BATTLE
OF NORMANDY, as the ignorant armies clash,
u dumbasses, the night is the one previous D-day,

the G.I. has snuck out of camp for one last
gutwrenching date with his girl.
probly he rented a room over a beach-bar
for a couple hours, the night is not stormy
like the ones previous so at dawn he'll enter hell.
when he's loosed his long line of spray
which is symbolic, he wants some air,
and calls her to the window, hes maybe

thinking of a greek-american buddy,
tough s.o.b., who maybe got killed in italy
maybe the word is greek for
so-fuck-less. the speaker knows he cld soon
have his dick shot off, or his head,
so no wonder he's sad, u dumbos,
gazing out at the mornful sea, his arm round
his tearful english doll in her girdle.

a sea of faith disapeared when WWII
dragged it's annoying ass self into play,
and espclly when america hit the beaches,
wch are fucked forever with shrapnel lieing around.

Arnolds is by now an old vet,
lookin back personaly thru the hellish haze
of omaha n all, to when he begged a doll stay true,
when nothin seemed true in the whole world.
this poem means a lot to me,

i may write more bout it so y'all should get your asses back over to read more ltr days.

Moth

Filling a jug with hot water
I saw a black flutter,
saw something leap.
A moth danced on the scalding water.
In my childhood I tore wings off flies.
Now I can hear the screams of scalded moths.

Shall I Compare You

Shall I compare you all to Doris Day?
You were as feminine and as temperate:
Your kisses lingering, as lilac may.
In time, but rarely on an early date,
You'd let me see your heavenly welts, the shine
Of clasps on straps, on soft flesh; but the dim
Recesses which those led to you'd decline
To show, although the hair you did not trim
Might possibly be felt...

But how it fades –
The memory of those girls to whom I owe
So much! They merely live as shades,
Like my young cock, that instantly would grow
Huge from a gleam of curves, wet from the sea,
While Keats or Shelley was entrancing me.

Learning to Translate

My sister exercising, trying to slim,
on the Melbourne lounge floor, grunt –
chuckling as she pedalled her legs,
her skirt rucked back, Ray,
the ex-RAAF navigator,
chuckling, and my parents too,
standing to one side;
and I not chuckling, but staring,
entranced, from straight in front of her,
at that moist, sweaty gusset and
the two-toned, tan nylon welts
easing, then taking
almost intolerable stress
from black straps, mesmerising
like the huge spider
I'd dropped the Family Bible on
before facing the blinding sun
on my way to High School.

Out of the blue, Ray –
who had looked down on blacked-out cities
suddenly blooming streets of fire
and exploding roses of death – cried
'Shoo! Shoo! go to your room!'
and blood rushing to my face
I left; and threw myself on my bed.
He could hardly have been angrier
with the Germans he'd bombed.
I must have done something terrible.
I tried to imagine what
mysteries lay behind
that black sweaty veil, which made it
so terrible to even see a few
black hairs each side… until,
failing helplessly, I modulated those
depths into the brooding, bewitching
opening piano chords of

that Rachmaninov Concerto
on Classical Favourites,
and black gigantic spiders.

Oxford Sabbatical

It felt like, twenty years before, my Viva.
Finding Bill with his mop, I mumbled out
'I had a guest, there's lots of blood…' Survivor
of Jap torpedoes, now a college scout,

Bill saw at once, his lizard face a mask,
This shy bloke who spent weekends with his wife
and kids had had a bint in. Didn't ask
whether her period caused it, or a knife.

'No problem, mate…' White sheets replaced the red.
He didn't blench that a girl bled so much,
so recently; for he could taste the blood-
streaked Java Sea, and feel the hidden clutch

of sharks on shipmates, too far gone to scream;
saw Nagasaki, from a camp offshore,
melt instantly. Now everything's a dream;
if needed, he would help get rid of her.

Cricket Lover

(rondeau redoublé)

He feels it still, the stroke that brought his ton;
No matter if he's reached his final score.
Though slower off the mark than anyone,
He must have had some talent at the core

As, round the time of Making Love not War,
Thinking, *the light won't last; good men have gone*,
He risked a pull that worked; then many more.
He feels it still, the stroke that brought his ton:

A rippling leg glide like a nylon's run!
'Some called me,' he says, 'selfish and cocksure,
But I have entertained, like Pietersen.'
No matter if he's reached his final score,

Which is around, he thinks, 124.
His flashing blade that once outscored the Don
Now blocks. And yet, from Kingston to Lahore,
Though slower off the mark than anyone,

He mastered every crease he played upon –
His old eyes twinkle at the metaphor;
But where's the flair and fire, caught off the sun,
He must have had? Some talent at the core

Glimmers, but like the sex drive of a nun.
Last, he corrects one piece of cricket lore,
That the great W.G. coached him at Wellington:
'Our School nurse, Grace, gave massage like a whore.
I feel it still.'

My Mistress' Eyes

My mistress' eyes scan nothing but the 'Sun';
Coral, her six-year-old, is better read;
She's had a boob-job that was badly done;
Her spiked, pink hair stops traffic far ahead;
At pool, straddling the cloth like Jimmy White,
She shows her thong bisecting heavy cheeks;
Pole-dancing twice a week, as 'Peach Delight',
She's drenched in oils and perfume till she reeks.
Ask her who Stalin was, she'll say *'Dunno'*;
When something good is on she'll drown the sound
With pointless chat, so that my mind must go
Into its own numb, switched-off Underground.
And yet our love is *filet mignon*, rare,
Since in the sack there's no one can compare.

Floods

I liked it when the river around our corner,
once every year or two, would start
to flood. Sandbags were laid at the doors,
we'd carry thermoses and food upstairs,
and wait to see if the Wye would come inside.
Nervous, excited, we all made jokes.

The nights were utterly silent, eerily still.
My wife and children slept, I'd stay awake
and every so often, at our bedroom window,
check how far the waters had reached
up our suburban avenue.

I'd see reflections of streetlights
stretching across the road to our front fence,
taut as violin strings; and feel the tug
of love, its mystery, confined for once
to what alone seemed real, my family.

Sweet Love, Renew thy Force

It was when I saw all the green expanse
Of England come into view over a roadside edge
That I knew the full joy of 'today'
And that it would not be dimmed by tomorrow:
Love returning to me in the form
Of your presence in all its fullness
And familiarity beside me again in my old car,
My spirit like a lark, and light perpetual
Embracing me, after the sad interim,
So seemingly permanent – you contracted
To another: now to see
Your love returning, making me more blessed,
A whole year's winter ice becoming
Miraculously that songfilled summer's day.

In Cimino's *The Deer Hunter*

In Cimino's *The Deer Hunter*
the captured Americans
are forced to play Russian roulette.
I am fascinated by
the convincing – but quite small –
change in their expression
when they lose.

Of course they are only acting.
The eyes of the shot deer
earlier in the film
glaze, and slide, no more
convincingly, yet somehow
with more conviction,
because the deer is not acting.

Travelling with a Photographer

We travel through a landscape charged
With images that strike home to his vision:
A granite rock, mud churned up, chicken pecking,
A fiery glow behind an engine-house
At night. A bear staring through bars. A window
Lit up as if to be a beacon for
Some youth who went off to America
A century ago. And through them runs
The thin thread of a red stream, the blood-flow
Of Cornwall, the beautiful bal-maiden.

The June sky's grey with just a ghost of blue,
A yellow stock-car's rusting in a field.
Near it, a clump of three or four
Granite cottages, a stiff un-neighbourly terrace,
Its quiet road vanishing into silence
And emptiness. There is nothing here
To make a living from or a life for.

'Do they have the same moon in America?'
Asked Auntie Perry, reading her brother's letter
From California: a fabled land, but more real
To her than Forest, where an alien tribe lived.
America, Australia, South Africa,
Might have a separate moon, but they were places
She'd seen in snaps sent home: those stiff and formal
Photos of miners in their Sunday-best,
Arms folded, smiling, heads cocked, cocksure.
No photos came from Forest or Condurrow.

Condurrow owns a man who owns a bear.
Twenty-five years he's kept it in his garage,
Feeding it golden syrup. My mind's like the bear's,
Driving through this country that's almost mine.
I pace the confines of a lock-up garage.
The brown bear lurks in all the photographs;
It shadows the tractor and red phone-booth at Bolenowe,

And yellow van sandwiched between cars.
The sea at Gwithian has iron bars.

Perhaps the bear, shambling hour after hour
In the dank, dark garage, breathing in
Motor-oil and turps, sees visions,
Senses the history of this place
In the way we see clouds drifting.
It sees the lightning-cloud of Wesley,
Miners and fishermen drunk with the spirit
Of the Lord. Now the chapel
So lovingly built and worshipped in
Is derelict, it's being sold off.
Where has the lightning-cloud gone?
Where's the spiritual fire?
It flickers, if anywhere, in the dim mind
Of a tamed and shaggy bear
Trapped in a garage.

My mother walked six miles to Tuckingmill
And back, each morning and evening. She'd have seen
The smoke and heard the grindings of
Dolcoath mine, but her mind was filled
With other images: images of love,
I guess; first love. I'd like an album
Filled with the photographs her pure
Imagination took, on just one journey
Of the thousands that she made. Yes, that would be
A startlingly beautiful anthology.
No artist, whether photographer or poet,
Could ever match the dazzle of her thoughts,
The day-dreams of a girl, setting off
For work in winter's dark, in spring and autumn's
Half-light, in the brilliance of summer.

The map we look at over a pub lunch
Shows No Man's Land. And I can imagine

The Red River landscape a setting for trench warfare.
It's never-ending; the salt, damp wind
Corrodes the windows and a man climbs his ladder
To undo the damage for a year or so; mud churns
To deeper mud that the pig snouts in.
He is a war correspondent, this photographer
Who drives me down narrow, winding lanes.
He's snapped the turmoil of the clouds
And frozen them into an illusion of calm.
And yet the very sharpness of the image
Moves them on in our minds, sends them drifting
Endlessly over the fields, unleashing showers
To churn more mud. His car tyres
Carry the mud churned-up by rain unleashed
By clouds captured in the slides he shows me.
A gentle man, he wields his camera like
A machete, making swathes through time.

And in the raw stump of a moment severed
From its neighbour, we glimpse the eternal
Now of a landscape none can photograph.

The Barbecue

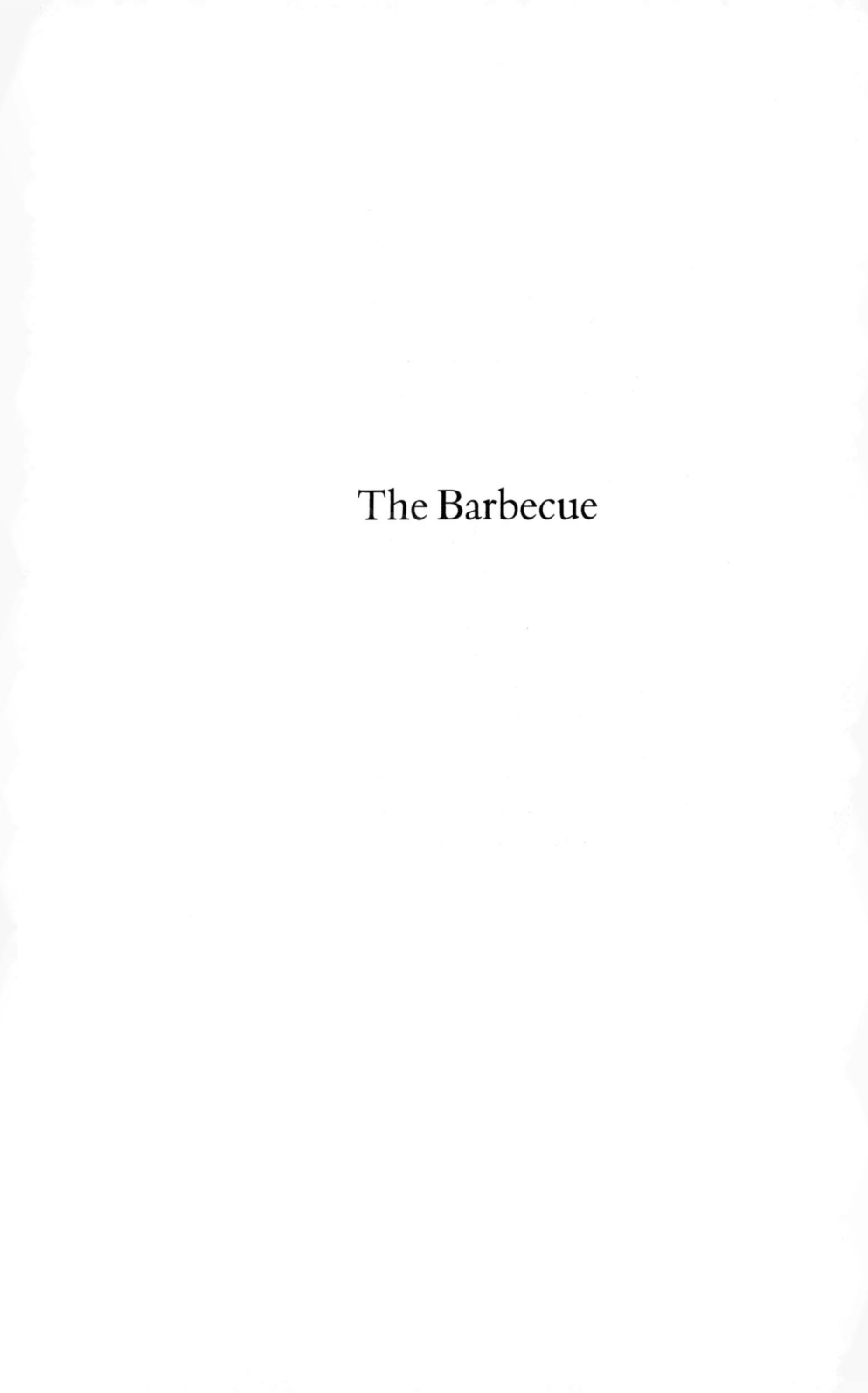

Suspender Belts

Suspender belts in a drawer in my study,
all tangled up, all black, some M and some L,
as she thickened with time;
one with a tiny red bow at the front.
Some are twenty or thirty years old, frayed.
They have never been moved for the last ten,
since I carried them, blindly weeping,
from our bedroom. I can't let them go.

I couldn't ask her friend to take them
to Oxfam, with all her other clothes;
besides, I can't see Zimbabwean girls in them.
They're of no use to anyone on earth.

Those clasps and buttons at the end
of the long straps won't trap the stockings
between them, with the deftness she knew
I never tired of; those little hooks and eyes
will never again be pulled together
by hands in the pit of her back, taking the strain.
In time they'll turn to dust, even the metals,
for they don't last as long as love does.

When Most I Wink

Things I miss: your tart laugh and seducing eyes,
The view of you rubbing your lips together
To even out your lipstick; in my sleep
Your bright darkness and your dark brightness merge
Into greyness – so I miss the shadow
Your womanly hips and slight breasts cast
On a clear summer's day, when you were happy
Tending the flowers you'd planted; your shade
Is still here; and I know I am blessed
That you still come, that I can still look at you,
However imperfectly; for we were never perfect,
Viewing each other as after a drugged sleep;
Drifted through love like sleepers in the night,
But now show our love clearly through my dreams.

Flight and Smoke

(For Tina, a Canadian student who asked me to shoot her for writing a 'bad sestina')

Your concern for my journey to Toronto is touching:
How will I bear the hours, unable to smoke?
The answer is, badly; alone up there with the sun,
Aware every moment of the terribly thin film
Between me and the start of the nothingness-flight
Through eternity… And there goes my tiny isle…

I go crazy if denied a seat by the aisle,
Squashed by gross bodies, and my knees touching
The seat in front; wedged as in space-flight
I pant for breath, it's like choking on smoke
Or being buried alive in a horror film.
The sweater I can't remove burns like the sun.

And then there's 9/11: is that a heavy sun-
Tan or… When he leaps up suddenly I'll
Hurl my pillow… I never watch the film,
Can't find the socket, women think I'm touching
Their thighs. Since, Jesus! I can't smoke,
I drink till stupefied in the droning flight.

The week will fly; before my homeward flight
I go to Kitchener to see my son,
His wife and stepchildren. I won't smoke
In their fresh new house. I hope I'll
Make contact; I have this odd fear of touching
My children. I must break through that film

That's like a lifetime's jetlag. Already, a film
Of sleepiness: reality put to flight
By an unnatural journey, our shadow touching
Greenland and Labrador, following the sun;
White landscapes cracked, isle after icy isle;
The lives I've left behind curl up in smoke.

I dip into Turgenev's novel, *Smoke*.
Then lights go out. Screen after screen, a trite film
Gapes at me as I lurch up and down the aisle,
In gaps between bad-tempered unisex flight-
Attendants' trolleys. Descent, tension, the late sun
Broods on Ontario's brown silence. Touching

Down now, I hope you're here to meet my flight.
Midnight for me, I lurch to dust and sun.
Okay, I'll shoot you. Afterwards, we smoke.

Through the Fens

Hot summer, a slow train through Cambridgeshire.
After one halt, a country woman sat
in my double-seat. Merged almost into her,
I saw, etched by her tautened dress on fat,
motherly fen-wife thighs, corset suspenders,
a resurrection, their chunky contours plain,
immense and unashamed. The lesser splendour,
Ely cathedral, slid past the dusty pane.

She drowsed, we swayed; the flatlands drifted by;
I ached to touch, as pilgrims draw the power
from healing relics – faint with desire
to let a sideways lurch propel my hand
to rest – 'I'm sorry!' – a moment on her thigh;
and she'd be moved by it, and understand.

Check-in, Milan Airport

Al cor gentil rempaira sempre amore
Come l'ausella in selva a la verdura...
'Did you pack your bags yourselves?'...
'No, Guido was there too – Guido Guinizelli.
And Dante, and Cavalcanti.'

To the gentle heart is love always returning
Like a bird to the green of a forest...
An Arab gentleman, having endured
A search by armed soldiers, obeys
A sign showing a figure in a skirt,
And hoists his robe in the ladies' toilet.

Liberal Westerners, trousered women, ignore
His privates-washing, though fearing he may be
Tucking away more than meets the eye.

He too, my wife reports, kept his eyes averted,
From modesty, and wishing he could vanish
From sight in this paranoid airport.
Everything is confused too in my heart.

Al cor gentil rempaira sempre amore
Come l'ausello in selva a la verdura...
Outside the plate glass, the great birds wait.
I'm carrying your image; no one spotted it.

An English Wedding in Provence

Geoff's an old mate of mine from the first school
        I taught at. I'm
Glad he's achieved his dream – the sun, the pool
Rita and he have finished just in time.
Their daughter's by it now, her wedding dress
Copied from Zeta Jones's, flicking off
Confetti as she eats a canapé.
Seeking a respite from the loud *jeunesse
Dorée*, who've flown for this from Stansted, Geoff
Confides to me his long-gone wedding day

In sleepy Lincolnshire... 'Our train was late
        Arriving, and we had
To reach our Bournemouth b & b by eight
Or there would be no dinner...' God, how sad
We were back then in postwar England! Full
Of roast beef and plum tart, he'd worried that
They wouldn't get their awful meal! He guessed
He found that small anxiety to dull
Those deeper: like, being squashed up in a flat
With babies and their puke; and first, the test

Of going all the way, that night in bed.
        Saw vests and pants
Submerged by bras and girdles when she said
The heat stuck her new roll-on to her. Aunts
Joked he'd soon pull it off. 'Christ, it was warm
That Whitsun, on that platform! We all dripped
With sweat, and wondered, where was the damned train.'
At last a rush of high heels and a swarm
Of hats like parrots, before their families slipped
Behind, small waving phantoms on the pane.

'I felt emotional, too overwrought
        To look at her.
Shit, this is it for life! That's how we thought.'
He breaks to thank a neighbour *pour les fleurs*.

Their rabbitoir, now chic and patio'd, glows
Gold in the fierce sun we sit huddling from
In a rare shade. They've planted cypresses
But they take time to grow. More champers flows,
More canapés, brought by the groom's mum –
Green trousersuit on which dim cows might graze.

    More pics, with Rita and the bride and groom.
        Then, sipping beer,
Geoff broods again: 'I felt a dreadful gloom
From Newark all the way to Hertfordshire,
And other wedding parties made it worse.
Today it's Marriage Lite, nothing profound.
This is his second wedding paid for by
The bride's dad, lucky sod! One fears divorce
And messed-up kids. I hope I'm not around
To pay for her next wedding. Matey, *I*

Should've cried just now in church! That dress – two grand
        It cost to make.
She's ordered the best wines tonight, best band…
They've been shacked-up for five years, for fucksake!
– Oh, *bonjour, Marc! Mathilde!*'… Not until
The evening, on the Abbey restaurant steps
In a quaint village, does he turn again
– After I've praised the *Lottes fraiches aux morilles*
And the exquisite *mélange* of small *crêpes*,
And lit a fag – to that hot 50s train.

He walked along the corridor, needing air,
        Great gulps of it.
As London densed, he'd felt close to despair.
He glimpsed a cricket-match, some chap's six-hit;
Then, in one carriage, a bald, solemn cove
In a dark suit and tie. Smoking, he bent
Over a notebook. He was on his own
– Incorrigibly so, deprived of love.

'You'll think I dream that, after the event;
But I sensed solitude in him like a stone,

And thought, O bugger! anything but such
            A tragic life!…
And really, all in all, there isn't much
I've missed out on; Rita's a great wife.
We're getting Sky, and friends will come each year.
Now the roof's done, we'll read. I shan't forget
The day I picked up a slim book of verse
In Hay on Wye, and saw that face appear:
The glasses, baldness, sadness, cigarette.
He married himself that day, for better or worse.'

Dachas

At the start of summer, out past the edge of Moscow,
Past the hidden haunts of Stalin, Rostropovich, Andropov,
The *intelligienti* arrive to breathe – after months of snow –
The country wildness, every Russian's first love.

They live, not by bread alone, nor money, but *blat*,
Near decent schools and clinics; and thank God,
However small and crammed their Moscow flat,
They're spared the mean existence of the *naród*.

A breed apart, before they've swept the mouldy *dacha*
They're gazing all round the overgrown gardens to see
Who's come back this year. 'Hi, Boris! Hi, Katya!'
All summer they will forget sin, forget memory.

Sunbathing by the beloved, muddy stream,
The son of a Party chief shot in the Lubyanka
And the gnarled old man who interrogated him
Discuss the latest play at the Taganka.

A great-niece of Dzerzhinsky, the murderous *Chekíst*,
Drinks tea with a doctor who killed only one soul
Simply by striking his own name from a death-list
Which meant another's was added to the roll.

For no one was completely innocent,
And freedom's not what it was thought to be;
They don't know where the twentieth century went,
That blizzard sweeping through us devilishly.

Bliny and vodka. Sweating from tennis on
        a pockmarked court,
Two young men, called Molotov and Chekhov,
And a beauty who sculpts when her hands don't abort,
Join the raucous outdoor party, talk about art and love.

The darkness throbbing with a single star, they clean
The dust off an ancient upright piano and someone plays
With exquisite feeling Rachmaninov and Scriabin,
Evoking meadows, peasants, gypsies, through
    a moist-eyed haze.

Blat: influence, 'knowing someone'; *naród*: the people; *Cheka*: precursor of the KGB; *bliny*: pancakes.

Images

1907

Lenin, in London for a Congress,
every morning dressed quickly
in his Kensington Square lodgings
pulled on his flat cap and hurried out
with one thought
in his icecold brain, one sight
in his piercing Tartar eyes:
the stall outside
King's Cross Station selling
the fish-and-chips he relished.

1949

On the Kolyma River,
reported the Soviet journal *Nature*,
a 'working party'
discovered a frozen stream
in the permafrost, containing
a perfectly preserved prehistoric
salamander. They hacked out the
30,000 year old fish from the ice,
thawed it and
devoured it straightaway
'with relish'.

The Barbecue

My soon-to-be fourth wife
is preparing for our first barbecue,
while my third wife
is taking out and packing books
she'd interwoven with mine
in alphabetical order.

Why is there always so much confusion?
My fourth wife is saying she brought twelve steak knives
from Canada, but now there are only nine.
I was hoping a certain poetry book
was mine, not my third wife's. I think
the barbecue tongs we will be using
are really hers.

I wish my third wife could stay for the barbecue
but my fourth wife would object,
and maybe my third wife would too.
I wish my first wife's second husband
would let her come to the barbecue,
and bring himself. My fourth wife
would be fine with that. Why are people
so unreasonable? I wish my second wife
wasn't dead, but could come too.
But then she wouldn't be happy with my third wife,
and my first wife not happy with my second.
I know my first wife would like my fourth wife.
Many hands make light work,
and I'm hopeless at this kind of thing –
getting the charcoal to light and
cooking chops, sausages and stuff.

Since You Came

So much late happiness in my head
Since you came into my life,
I feel like an over-gifted child:
like little Petya Tchaikovsky, aged five,
beating his head against a window pane
crying, 'I've got all this music in me!'
You've given me so much joy, it's pain;
Yet still I want that melody again.

Cloudburst

Somehow I always miss the moodswing when
Threads that have hovered lowly in the west
– Wispy and tiny, flecks of albumen,
Fated to disappear or stay at rest
Because the sky is the same blue it's been
For many weeks, so that I almost want
An interruption and a change of scene,
Though really, in my heart of hearts, I don't –
Have turned, without my seeing, to grey clouds,
To a black mass, cascading savage rain,
And what has been serene instantly shrouds;
I fear for us, fear nothing will remain.
Brief madness; but your tears are the only way
You have to shock me back to us, you say.

'I never died, said he…'

i.m. J D-S

Well, now, old friend, you won't have to worry about
How you'll find, in your sixties, young Katya's
School fees, or feel the slight pain in your chest
And slight panic in your mind when
Lena comes bursting back into the chaotic flat
Carrying a Harrods' shopping bag and
Exclaiming, in her Russian accent, 'Jo, Jo,
I've saved us lot of money!'

You won't have to worry about touting for business
From editors, or slaving over your latest impeccable
Article, so you can pay the month-before-last's
Rent on the expensive flat, and the expensive
Life Insurance. It can be cashed in now; your payments
Are over. You can rest from your labours, old friend,
Old greybearded friend, built like a Russian bear
And with a bear's hug for your *druzyá*.

You won't be rushing to market for the right meat
And veg to cook for the stream of Russian brigands
Counting on you for a free week in London,
Nor lugging the carrierfuls of red wine for them.
Lena would say, 'Jo, you must write bestseller.'

No wonder you made a film about the Kalashnikov,
But you loved her exceedingly, your Slav princess.
You won't have to think up the long emotional toasts
To wives, women, beauty, friendship, Russia.
You won't have to play for me, every time I came,
Paul Robeson singing '*Dzo Kheell*' in Stalin's Moscow,

So we could sing, '*I dreamed last night I saw Joe Hill
Alive as you and me…*' Jo, I've seen and heard you
So often since I learned of your aneurysm; and since
I heard today you were dead I've kept singing to myself

'*Says Joe, But I ain't dead...*' And Jo, you're not dead;
'*Says Joe, I never died...*' Jo, you never died;
With your wry, kind smile and twinkling baggy eyes,
Your hand still holding a ghostly cigarette,
You're saying, 'I'm sorry, all I have left is love.'

After Christopher Smart

For I will consider my dog Tamsin,
For she appearath round the corner of the house
When we are drinking wine outside, then stops,
Forgetting why she appeareth there;
For she is 108 years old in human terms,
For she is almost blind and almost deaf,
Yet suddenly she trotteth down the garden,
For then her tail wags upon prink, in joy of living,
So that I have started to call her Baron von Trott;
For then she will slow up and plod around the house
Four or five times, defending it from marauders,
For she is small in size but mighty in spirit,
For when she stumbleth over a root, or her back legs
Won't work, she still goeth bravely forward;
For when we put some tasty fish in her dish,
She will slowly stir from her basket
And plod to her dish; but then she pauseth
For a long time, saying her prayers to the Lord,
Calling down blessing on the food,
Before suddenly stooping her head and
Snatching the fish hungrily.
For she kicketh out her legs in her dreams,
For she loveth to run on a beach,
And dreams of it later, many times,
Though she feareth the water.
For she is a happy little dog,
And teacheth how to grow old gracefully;
For she is the handmaid of the Lord,
And hath been loved by a Master and three Mistresses.
For she knoweth no other life but with us.

Sunday Morning on Madeira

The dogs are singing; it's their own chorale
suddenly starts up from all around
our hotel balcony,
tenors and basses, and one lone falsetto,
it mounts to a crescendo, it's like Bartok
and a steel band, savage and beautiful
celebrating life and their Creator
even in their own cramped, squalid ghetto.
The sea is listening to this joyous sound;
and when it stops as suddenly as it started,
out of the stunned silence a cock,
alone and apart,
chanticleers proudly, 'Now this is art'.

Air Excess

Have you flown with Air Excess?
I did so recently;
It's an experience you shouldn't miss.
Soon as the plane is in the air,
The passengers light up joyfully,
And everyone's disposed to share,
In the old Cary Grant-ish way,
Saying to others 'Would you care
For a Rothman?'... 'Have a Sobranie!'
Hostesses in their underwear
(Stockings, suspenders *de rigueur*)
Pass round champagne, and fluted glasses;
The whole cabin's in a roar,
The captain, shirt in disarray,
Appears and leads a merry song.
*'Thank God we're leaving the UK.
We're free!'* Glasses are being clinked
From row to row, or smashed
To celebrate some couple's wedding
– They're copulating in the aisle
While people watch admiringly
And shout Bravo! All arms are linked,
And everyone's completely smashed.
We don't know where
The flight is heading and don't care.
The moon, perhaps. And it's so cheap!
Food's extra, a few quid, but nice,
Like Helford oysters served on ice.
There's shameless swapping between seats:
People who've never dared to stray
From their dull marriages entwine
With strangers; no one gives a toss,
Being on an Excess holiday,
Staid matrons are seen licking wine
From unzipped rampant cocks and balls,
And their staid husbands don't look cross,
Lost in an ecstasy of cunt.

It's even wilder at the front,
With threes and fours mixed up (the space
More generous in Club Excess).
Ten quid for Gatwick to Moldova,
And taking in Niagara Falls,
That's all I paid, plus airport tax,
And wished it to be never over;
I really started to relax.
Book your flight – you'll have a bomb!
Google AirExcess.com

Three Triolets

Obby Oss

That bashful girl I have to pull
Under my whirling cloak this Mayday.
Though some who push are beautiful
That bashful girl I have to pull.
You troubadours of love, so full
Of artful, pleasing dances, *m'aidez*!
That bashful girl I have to pull
Under my whirling cloak this Mayday.

Latin Class

I fell in love with Sara's nape,
Between her short black hair and collar.
Tonguetied and ugly as an ape,
I fell in love with Sara's nape,
Its coolness, whiteness, slender shape;
She never knew I was its scholar.
I fell in love with Sara's nape,
Between her short black hair and collar.

Vermeer's Milkmaid

She hides her happiness or tears
As she pours milk out of the pitcher;
Though she's been dead 300 years,
She hides her happiness or tears;
No art is greater than Vermeer's,
Yet her small life is greater, richer.
She hides her happiness or tears,
As she pours milk out of the pitcher.

Centenary Thanksgiving for Thomas Merritt

'Order of Service: Please **stand** as the Dean conducts the
Deputy Lieutenant... to her seat at the front of the nave...'

(Truro Cathedral, June 2008).

'Do 'ee mind if I sit here a minute, my 'andsome?'
I was on a bench, smoking, before the walk home.
He sat; the crowd was still streaming out
and past us, silent, sober, in the mild evening light.
He pointed to the Order of Service in my lap:
'I still haven't got over the first shock. Stand *up*!

– stand up for *they*! I'd have turned in my grave
if I'd been in it; when they wafted up the nave
it was like they was puttin' we simple folk in our place,
tampin' down the mood and the spirit, in case
"*Hark the glad sound!*" sparked off an explosion
of full-voiced, rapturous, Cornish emotion.

Like Billy Bray, I never stood up for anyone;
and do'ee know why? – because I am a King's son!
Worship, for we, was like the blasting of rocks
in the bal, not that row of pasty-faced men in frocks
who kept us flat, like a drizzle on Carn Brea,
by getting up and bleating in turn, with nothin' to say.

They'd 'a' been throwed from the pulpit home Redruth
– or more likely, chucked off the cliff at Hell's Mouth.
And where was the thunder of triumphant Calvary
in the Bible readings? Wisht as gnats' wee,
it hurt me to hear it! Somebody must have sieved
all the glory out, like they wanted to say He never lived –
the Infant Stranger, Jesse's tender rod! I tell 'ee, boy,
it felt like a museum; with less joy

than there was in my hovel with sand on the floor
when I called for a pen to write down one more
heavenly tune before I went – one more Hosanna!
And I've heard my curls from Moonta to Montana

sung with ecstasy by crowds of Cousin Jacks,
deep underground, or in chapels no more'n shacks,
but as to that gilded prison there, I thirst
for the hour when *"the gates of brass before Him burst,*
The iron fetters yield!"... Well, see 'ee 'gain,
my lover.' He shuffled off down St Mary's Lane,

warbling, in both contralto and baritone,
"The glorious Lord,
    the glorious Lord,
        of Life comes down,
Of Life comes down!"... a crazy tramp who grieved
for majestic words, and preachers who believed,
and thought he was poor Tom, down a mine at eleven,
his body clamped by pain, his head in heaven.

Thomas Merritt (1863-1908), frail, self-taught musician and composer of famous Christmas carols.
Billy Bray (1794-1868), miner and inspirational preacher. 'Bal' - mine; 'wisht' - weak; 'curls' -carols.

Easter Reading

We went at Easter to hear my old friend Peter Redgrove
read at a college. He was already in full flow,
that strong bald head, that resonant, calm voice.
The hall was full, the students attentive;
soon he was saying, *I'll just read one more poem.*

I found him afterwards outside, standing apart,
smoking. I said I was sorry we'd arrived
late, but we'd not expected him to start
so promptly. He said, *well, they're Buddhists, you see,*
(with a characteristic dry chuckle
I'd forgotten over the years)
and you have to get on with it!

I said, scanning the crowd sitting on steps
around us, *Denise is here somewhere,
looking for you, have you seen her?* Then realised
Denise is dead. And the pain of that woke me
before I could tell him my mistake, then
I realised Peter is dead, so I didn't need to tell him.

I padded along to my study to record
the dream in the stillness of the night,
and a few lines ago something fell or was thrown,
a flicker of light, I heard it bounce.
When I looked it was a lightbulb, unbroken.

Changing the Flowers

A jokey byword for meanness and sourness,
our Doris: untouching and untouchable,
visited at all only because
people loved her dead daughter.
Born to the dirt-poor pre-war East End,
St Vitus' Dance ended her schooling;
not stupid, though she still believed,
in labour, babies came out at the navel.

She's had a bad word for all – even Shakespeare,
who 'couldn't have been much good
because he only wrote one book'.
Her bleak, pictureless bungalow
stuffed with bags of banknotes, she gave
her cleaner last Christmas her old hairbrush,
white hairs still tangled in it.

Utterly unspiritual,
yet was granted one strange encounter
in mid-life when, hired as
an office cleaner, on her first evening
she saw, through the glass screen into
another office, in fading light, a lady
changing the flowers in vases.
Asked who she was the next day;
the typists turned pale, and said,
'That's what Mrs Carbis always did,
every evening. She loved putting in
fresh flowers. Her funeral is tomorrow.'

Now Doris herself is ghosting, slowly,
her leg rotting; yet a kind of *joie de vivre*
we've only glimpsed in wedding snaps,
before George turned alcoholic and
prone to mad violence, lights up her face;
she loves the nurses stroking her,
says to us, 'Have you enough money?

Take whatever you want!'… 'Tomorrow
a famous artist is coming to paint the ward!'
We don't know who this lady is
who in the fading light, through a glass darkly,
is changing the flowers.

A Kind of Relative

In the night, this time, it was no confused old man
who intruded on you. Coming for your things,
we are surprised to find you still in your sunny room,
your mouth gaping from the surprise of being dead.

You look no different from when we'd visit
and find you drowsing, mouth open. It's so new,
you ought to be able to say *something*. Perhaps
'Denise came by!' or 'Did you bring my nightie?'

We never touched, just as I won't touch you now;
I stand well back, as I always did, until
we had to bend over you and shout
to rouse you. What if I came close, shouted your name?…

You wanted to die in your silent, decaying house.
Stubborn cow, in the end you slept in your own shit,
pulled yourself round your kitchen on your bum.
Lately we found you this nice Home, nice room.

And as a poet almost said, a Home is where,
if they'll take you in, you have to go there.
I'm surprised that I don't like you being dead
just as much as I didn't like you, living.

I don't feel grief, exactly, for this mother-in-law
from a death, ten years and two marriages ago;
there should be a word for it,
as Eskimos have words for different kinds of snow.

Mad Fathers

I am drawn to the daughters of mad fathers,
And they to me. I am the rock
On which this frail but gutsy flock
Of stormy petrels gathers,
Safe in knowing that I am only half-mad.
Some even think me not half-bad
In bed, since I remind them of their fathers,
Loved despite all – unlike their mothers,

Who they think are to blame, more or less,
For their dads' craziness – cold, reserved,
Terrified of passion, preserved
By unfailing righteousness.
I am the Rockall in the turbulent Atlantic,
A bleak haven for their frantic
Distress cries, and when we have sex
They are troubled, cold, passionate, complex:

Since through me they are fucking their dad,
And saying fuck-you to their mum.
They're not disturbed if we don't come,
Preferring, like me, a constant tension
Reminding them of their childhood home.
As do – but mildly – my hypochondria,
My distance, my erotomania,
My life half real and half invention.

I am drawn to the daughters of cold mothers
And mad fathers, who could be genial jokers
In a pub, then turn on their wives with pokers,
Every one a whore, a multiple adulteress;
Their genteel houses just a shell,
Like the stark walls of war-torn Stalingrad.
The daughters ask little of me: to be half-mad;
They don't need too much happiness.

Schrödinger's Cat

Schrödinger's famous paradox
Says that though particles may be
Dead *and* alive till someone looks,
Only an idiot could say
A cat, shut in a soundproof box,
Is dead – *and* miaowing plaintively.

'But if the two are linked together,
By poison, say,' he gaily wrote,
'You have to ask the question whether
Cat can be dead, electron not –
Rather, not one state nor the other.'
Around the globe his question shot.

He wandered in that spacious park
That's not with glades and fountains set,
But neutron, positron and quark
(Which hadn't been discovered yet),
But also loved the human spark
Of a shy glance one can't forget.

It's said a late erotic passion
Led to his Nobel Prize,
Deep intellectual creation
Springing from some girl's eyes,
A sense that everything's wave motion
From joy between her thighs.

And Schrödinger, he kept two wives
In his *gemütlich* flat;
He had to hide the kitchen knives
For each could be a cat;
Each day one fades, the other thrives,
And what's the harm in that?

In time the complications grew;
Prim Princeton tried to bring him over;

They'd take his wives; a colleague too;
But jibbed when someone blew his cover,
Revealing a still headier brew –
The colleague's wife was Erwin's lover.

Into his life without a care
Sauntered the swastika rat;
Nobody knew why Schrödinger
Became a Cheshire cat
Who both was there and was not there –
But what's the harm in that?

That the whole cosmos was one Mind
Increasingly he thought;
But as to what might be behind
The dark – infinity or nought –
The brilliant physicist of Light
Was like us, blind.

He thought all politics a bore,
Loved sitting in the sweet Tyrole
With brilliant friends, where talk could soar,
Smoking his pipe, his head aswirl
From the delicious *heuringer*
Served by a buxom girl.

Say this for him: that he survived
In our inconsequent miracle;
The paradox is being alive,
Whether as wave or particle;
The cats-eyes shining as we drive
Say life is nothing, and life is all.

Schrödinger (1887–1961) publicly welcomed the *Anschluss*, then, full of remorse, fled from Austria. '*Heuringer*', last year's vintage.

Plain Song

Perfect, cloudless day, such as we only get
Two or three times in a year,
And a bird somewhere, like a throbbing clarinet
Starts a sweet Broadway song I ought to know
Yet maddeningly don't. But here's a phrase
'Now listen, sister,' from 'fish gotta swim…'
Then another, husky: 'If I loved you…' It's clear
The birds are ravished by these sun-drenched days
As I am, and they've heard so many musicals
Through our windows, through the wind and rain,
The same life-giving songs time and again,
They've learnt the pauses and the intervals.
They leave the words to me, and all the pain
And joy of love. They sing it plain.